THIS BOOK BELONGS TO...

DEDICATION

To _ _ _ _ _ _ _ _ _ _ _ _ _ _ _ _
My Mom

You are the strongest person i will ever know. You example, your accomplishments, and your determination have been the lessons of my life.

Thank you for all of it.

I Love You Mom

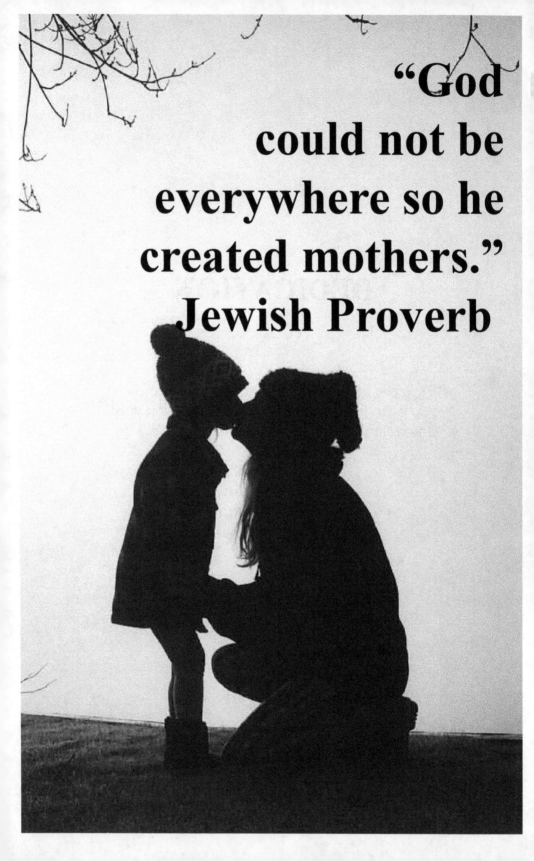

Mom, What's Your Story

IT'S YOUR BIRTHDAY!

"Life began with waking up and loving my mother's face."
George Eliot

1. What is your birthdate?

___

2. What was your full name at birth?

___

3. Were you named after a relative or someone else of significance?

___

___

4. In what city were you born?

___

5. Were you born in a hospital? If not, where?

___

___

6. What were your first words?

___

___

7. How old were your parents when you were born?

___

___

Mom, What's Your Story
IT'S YOUR BIRTHDAY!

"All that I am or ever hope to be, I owe to my angel mother."
Abraham Lincoln

8. What was your height (lenght) and weight at birth?

_____

9. Were you the oldest, middle, or youngest child? How many siblings do you have?

_____

_____

10. What have your parents told you about how you were as a baby?

_____

_____

_____

_____

_____

_____

_____

_____

_____

_____

_____

Mom, What's Your Story

Mom, What's Your Story

IT'S YOUR BIRTHDAY!

"Life doesn't come with a manual, it comes with a mother."
Unknown

11. What stories have you been told about the day you were born?

_____
_____
_____
_____
_____
_____
_____
_____
_____
_____
_____
_____
_____
_____
_____

Mom, What's Your Story

Mom, What's Your Story

IT'S YOUR BIRTHDAY!

"A mother is she who can take the place of all others but whose place no one else can take." - Cardinal Meymillod

12. What is your earliest childhood memory?

Mom, What's Your Story

Mom, What's Your Story

Mom, What's Your Story

Mom, What's Your Story

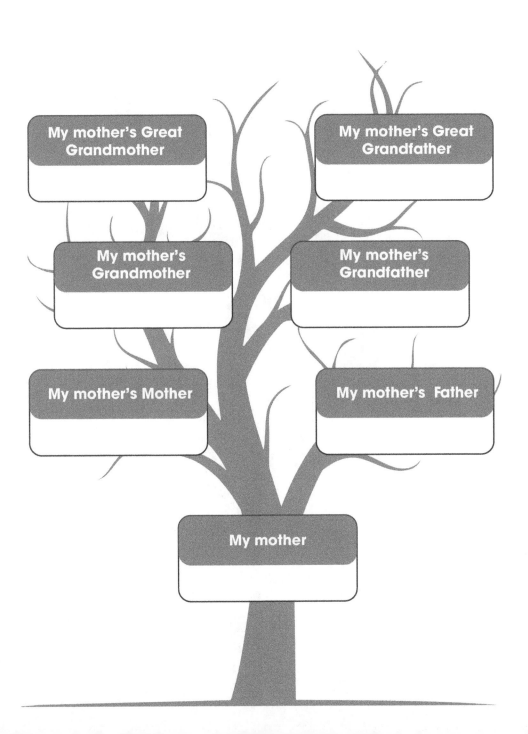

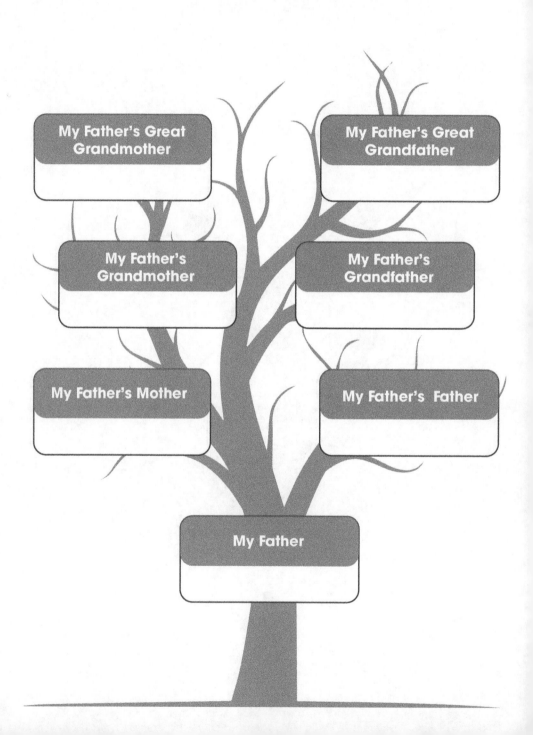

Mom, What's Your Story

GROWING UP

"A mother's love endures through all."
Washington Irving.

1. Where did you grow up when you were a kid?

___

___

2. Did you have a nickname?

___

3. Is There a television show you remember loving to watch?

___

___

4. What were your regular chores?

___

___

5. Did you get an allowance? If yes, how much?

___

___

6. Who was your best friend?

___

___

___

Mom, What's Your Story

GROWING UP

"The natural state of motherhood is unselfishness."
Jessica Lange.

7. What do you miss most about being a kid?

_____
_____
_____
_____

8. What were you like when you were a kid?

_____
_____
_____
_____

9. What was the worst trouble you remember getting into as a kid?

_____
_____
_____
_____
_____
_____

Mom, What's Your Story

GROWING UP

"The natural state of motherhood is unselfishness."
Jessica Lange.

10. What was your favorite candy when you were a kid?

_____

_____

_____

_____

_____

_____

_____

_____

_____

_____

_____

_____

_____

_____

_____

Mom, What's Your Story

Mom, What's Your Story

Mom, What's Your Story

Mom, What's Your Story

Mom, What's Your Story

WHERE HAVE YOU LIVED?

"Anyone can live in a house, but homes are created with patience, time and love." Jane Green

List the cities you have lived in during your life. Include the dates if you can remember them.

Mom, What's Your Story

Mom, What's Your Story

Mom, What's Your Story

Mom, What's Your Story

THE TEENAGE YEARS

"The best place to cry is on a mother's arms."
Jodi Picoult

1. How did you dress and style your hair during your teens? Do you have any pictures?

___
___
___
___
___
___
___
___
___
___
___
___
___
___
___

Mom, What's Your Story

THE TEENAGE YEARS

"The best place to cry is on a mother's arms."
Jodi Picoult

2. Did you hang out with a group of people or a small number of close friends? Do you still talk to any of them?

_____
_____
_____
_____
_____
_____
_____
_____
_____
_____
_____
_____

3. In what kind of car did you learn to drive?

_____
_____

4. Who taught you to drive?

_____
_____

Mom, What's Your Story

THE TEENAGE YEARS

"A mother is not a person to lean on, but a person to make leaning unnecessary." Dorothy Canfield Fisher

5. What was a common weekend night like during your teens?

_____

_____

_____

_____

_____

_____

_____

_____

_____

_____

_____

_____

_____

_____

_____

_____

Mom, What's Your Story

THE TEENAGE YEARS

"A mother is not a person to lean on, but a person to make leaning unnecessary."   Dorothy Canfield Fisher

6. Knowing all you know now, what advice would you give your teenage self?

Mom, What's Your Story

Mom, What's Your Story

THE TEENAGE YEARS

"If I have done anything in life worth attention, I feel sure that I inherited the disposition from my mother."
Booker T. Washington

7. Describe what you were like during your teen years.

_____

_____

_____

_____

_____

_____

_____

_____

_____

_____

_____

_____

_____

_____

_____

_____

Mom, What's Your Story

Mom, What's Your Story

THE TEENAGE YEARS

"If I have done anything in life worth attention, I feel sure that I inherited the disposition from my mother."
Booker T. Washington

8. Write about a favorite memory from your teens.

_____
_____
_____
_____
_____
_____
_____
_____
_____
_____
_____
_____
_____
_____
_____
_____
_____
_____

Mom, What's Your Story

Mom, What's Your Story

"FEW things are more delightful than grandchildren fighting over your lap."
Doug larson

Mom, What's Your Story

WHAT HAPPENED THE YEAR YOU WERE BORN?

"I remember my mother's prayers and they have always followed me. They have clung to me all my life."
Abraham Lincoln

Google the following for the year you were born:

1. What historical events occurred?

_____
_____
_____
_____
_____
_____
_____

2. What movie won the academy award for best picture? Who won best Actor and best Actress?

_____
_____
_____

3. What were a few popular movies that came out the year you were born?

_____
_____
_____

Mom, What's Your Story

WHAT HAPPENED THE YEAR YOU WERE BORN?

"Life began with waking up and loving my mother's face." George Eliot

4. What song was on the top of the Billboard charts?

_____

_____

5. Who was the President of the United States?

_____

6. What were a few popular television shows?

_____

_____

_____

7. What were the prices for the following items?

- A loaf of bread: _____
- A gallon of milk: _____
- A cup of coffee: _____
- A dozen eggs: _____
- The average cost of a few home: _____
- A first-class stamp: _____
- A new car: _____
- A gallon of gas: _____
- A movie ticket: _____

Mom, What's Your Story

Mom, What's Your Story

Mom, What's Your Story

Mom, What's Your Story

Mom, What's Your Story

Mom, What's Your Story

Mom, What's Your Story

Mom, What's Your Story

WHAT KIND OF STUDENT WERE YOU?

"There's no way to be a perfect mother and a million ways to be a good one." — Jill Churchill

1. What did you like and dislike about school?

_____
_____
_____
_____

2. What kind of grades did you get?

_____
_____

3. What were your favorite and least favorite subjects?

_____
_____
_____
_____
_____

Mom, What's Your Story

WHAT KIND OF STUDENT WERE YOU?

"I realized when you look at your mother, you are looking at the purest love you will ever know."
Mitch Albom

4. What was your relationship with your parents like during your high school years?

___

Mom, What's Your Story

WHAT KIND OF STUDENT WERE YOU?

"I realized when you look at your mother, you are looking at the purest love you will ever know."
Mitch Albom

5. Did you play any sports?

_____

_____

6. What were the school activities that you participated in?

_____

_____

_____

_____

_____

_____

_____

_____

_____

_____

WHAT KIND OF STUDENT WERE YOU?

"I realized when you look at your mother, you are looking at the purest love you will ever know."
Mitch Albom

7. Is there a teacher or coach that had a significant impact on you? What was their biggest influence?

_____
_____
_____
_____
_____
_____
_____
_____
_____
_____
_____
_____
_____
_____
_____

Mom, What's Your Story

Mom, What's Your Story

Mom, What's Your Story

Mom, What's Your Story

Mom, What's Your Story

BECOMING A MOM

"Being a mother is an attitude, not a biological relation."
Robert A. Heinlein

1. How old were you when you first became a mother?

___

2. Who was the first person you told that you were going to be a mom?

___

3. Is there a specific song you would sing to your kids when they were little?

___

4. What is the biggest difference in how kids are raised today and when you raised your kids?

___

Mom, What's Your Story

BECOMING A MOM

"If evolution really works, how come mothers only have two hands?" Milton Berle

5. Is there anything you would change about how kids were raised?

_____
_____
_____
_____
_____
_____
_____
_____
_____
_____
_____
_____
_____
_____
_____

Mom, What's Your Story

BECOMING A MOM

"If evolution really works, how come mothers only have two hands?" Milton Berle

6. What is the biggest difference in your childhood and that of kids today?

_____
_____
_____
_____
_____
_____
_____
_____
_____
_____
_____
_____
_____
_____

Mom, What's Your Story

BECOMING A MOM

"If evolution really works, how come mothers only have two hands?" Milton Berle

7. Knowing what you know now, what advice would you give yourself as a new mother?

_____
_____
_____
_____
_____
_____
_____
_____
_____
_____
_____
_____
_____
_____
_____
_____

Mom, What's Your Story

Mom, What's Your Story

Mom, What's Your Story

Mom, What's Your Story

Mom, What's Your Story

MOM TRIVIA

"Most mothers are instinctive philosophers."
Harriet Beecher Stowe

1. What is your favorite flavor of ice cream?
   _____

2. How do you like your coffee?
   _____

3. How do you like your eggs cooked?
   _____
   _____

4. What is the eye color for each of your kids?
   _____

5. Do you still have your tonsils?
   _____

6. What is your shoe size?
   _____

7. What is your favorite season?
   _____

8. Do you have any allergies?
   _____

Mom, What's Your Story

MOM TRIVIA

"(A) mother is one to whom you hurry when you are troubled." Emily Dickinson

9. What would you pick as your last meal?
_____
_____

10. Have you ever collected anything during your life?
_____
_____

11. Preference: cook or clean ?
_____
_____

12. Were you a Girl Scout?
_____
_____

13. What do you do better than anyone else in you family?
_____
_____
_____
_____

Mom, What's Your Story

Mom, What's Your Story

Mom, What's Your Story

Mom, What's Your Story

Mom, What's Your Story

Mom, What's Your Story

Mom, What's Your Story

MORE SONGS ABOUT MOMS

"There's no way to be a perfect mother and a million ways to be a good one."   Jill Churchill

- "Mother" by Kacey Musgraves
- "The Perfect Fan" by The Backstreet Boys
- "What Mama Say (Life Is Good)" by Jason Mra
- "Turn to You" by Justin Bieber
- "Ring Off" by Beyoncé
- "Mom" by Meghan Trainor featuring Kelli Trainor
- "Mama" by Spice Girls
- "Mother" by Sugarland
- "Like My Mother Does" by Lauren Alaina
- "Don't Forget to Remember Me" by Carrie Underwood
- "Dear Mama" by Tupac
- "In My Daughter's Eyes" by Martina McBride
- "The Hand That Rocks the Cradle" by Glen Campbell and Steve Wariner
- "Mama Tried" by Merle Haggard
- "Mama Said" by Metallica
- "Mom" by Meghan Trainor (featuring Kelli Trainor)
- "Oh Mother" by Christina Aguilera

Mom, What's Your Story

MORE SONGS ABOUT MOMS

"A mother is not a person to lean on, but a person to make leaning unnecessary."
Dorothy Canfield Fisher

- "Mama's Song" by Carrie Underwood
- "Somebody's Hero" by Jamie O'Neal
- "Ring Off" by Beyoncé
- "Promise to Try" by Madonna
- "Mother Like Mine" by The Band Perry
- "A Song for Mama" by Boyz II Men
- "I'll Be There" by Mac Miller
- "Baby Mama" by Fantasia
- "Tough" by Craig Morgan
- "I'll Always Love My Mama" by The Intruders
- "Mama Knows" by Shenandoah
- "The Mother" by Brandi Carlile
- "My Mother & I" by Lucy Dacus
- "Two of Us" by Louis Tomlinson
- "Ring Off" by Beyoncé
- "Coat of Many Colors" by Dolly Parton
- "A Song for Mama" by Boyz II Men

Mom, What's Your Story

NOTES

NOTES

Mom, What's Your Story

NOTES

Mom, What's Your Story

NOTES

Mom, What's Your Story

NOTES

Mom, What's Your Story

NOTES

Mom, What's Your Story

NOTES

Mom, What's Your Story

NOTES

Mom, What's Your Story

NOTES

Mom, What's Your Story

NOTES

Mom, What's Your Story

NOTES

Mom, What's Your Story

NOTES

Mom, What's Your Story

NOTES

Mom, What's Your Story

NOTES

Mom, What's Your Story

NOTES

Mom, What's Your Story

NOTES

Mom, What's Your Story

NOTES

Mom, What's Your Story

NOTES

Mom, What's Your Story

NOTES

Mom, What's Your Story

NOTES

Mom, What's Your Story

NOTES

Mom, What's Your Story

NOTES

Mom, What's Your Story

NOTES

Mom, What's Your Story

NOTES

Mom, What's Your Story

NOTES

Mom, What's Your Story

NOTES

Mom, What's Your Story

NOTES

Mom, What's Your Story

NOTES

Mom, What's Your Story

NOTES

Mom, What's Your Story

NOTES

Mom, What's Your Story

NOTES

Mom, What's Your Story

NOTES

Mom, What's Your Story

NOTES

Mom, What's Your Story

NOTES

www.ingramcontent.com/pod-product-compliance
Lightning Source LLC
LaVergne TN
LVHW012214181224
799472LV00035B/1118